Moment?
to Remember

Brad,

With my prayers as you
support others as they reflect
on the God-touched moments of
life — Carol Ann, SND

Brad!

By God's grace we
met in 1967 before you
entered "this least society."
May this book deepen your awareness
of God's love for you, presence and
action in your life NOW and as
you help our brothers grow older
gracefully — pondering Moments to Remember

Gene, sj

Moments
to Remember

Ignatian Wisdom for Aging

Carol Ann Smith, SHCJ and Eugene F. Merz, SJ

New City Press
of the Focolare
Hyde Park, NY

Published in the United States by New City Press
202 Comforter Blvd., Hyde Park, NY 12538
www.newcitypress.com
© 2015 Carol Ann Smith, SHCJ and Eugene F. Merz, SJ

Cover design by Leandro De Leon
Layout by Steven Cordiviola

Library of Congress Cataloging-in-Publication Data

Smith, Carol Ann
   Moments to remember : Ignatian wisdom for aging / by Carol Ann
Smith, SHCJ and Eugene F. Merz, SJ.
      pages cm
   Summary: "This book responds to the hunger for purpose among the
aging. Tapping into the tradition of Ignatian spirituality it offers some
of the wisdom of the Christian story as found in the parables and
conversations of Jesus. It provides encouragement for aging, and a way
to share the experience"—Provided by publisher.
   ISBN 978-1-56548-574-7 (alk. paper)
   1. Aging—Religious aspects—Christianity. 2. The Spiritual Exercises of
St. Ignatius. I. Merz, Eugene. II. Title.
   HQ1061.S573 2015
   270.084'6--dc23
                                        2015005146

Printed in the United States of America

DEDICATION

In gratitude for our parents

Alice C. and Frank C. Merz
Margaret K. and Paul W. Smith

who taught us a grateful love for the world
and hope for its children.

Contents

PART II

PART III

PART IV

PREFACE

*O*ur lives are filled with companions — all providentially given to us on our journey home to God. Each companion plays a special role and some, though residing in the background, still offer support and aid us in the on-going challenge to live in a balanced and discerning way. This book aims to be just such a companion. It is simple in format, friendly in approach and one to be picked up day by day as the seasons of life unfold. We envision a person taking it up in the morning or the evening — perhaps daily, perhaps on a few days of the week. It may be used in conjunction with daily scripture readings. It may even find a role in your conversations with others. Above all, it is a book to be prayed, not a book simply to be read.

As current generations of the American population age, we are offered some new challenges and some new possibilities. We are keenly aware that as better health may give us longer lives, it will also offer us continuing opportunities to grow and develop in faith, hope and love. As our life is further enriched by experiences that are multi-generational and multi-cultural, we will need to find simple, effective actions that allow our diversity to be reverenced and used as the strength God surely intends. This may be a new moment for capitalizing upon the wisdom of the elders. Our lives are filled with Moments to Remember. Sharing with others the fruit of one's prayer with this little book may contribute to this new moment.

It was after we had almost completed our writing this book that Pope Francis was elected pope of the Catholic Church. In so many ways his words and actions resonate with many of the themes in this book. Above all, his view of the elders among us touched a chord in us.

> Whenever we attempt to read the signs of the times it is helpful to listen to young people and the elderly. Both represent a source of hope for every people. The elderly bring with them memory and the wisdom of experience, which warns us not to foolishly repeat our past mistakes. Young people call us to renewed and expansive hope, for they represent new directions for humanity and open us up to the future....
>
> *Pope Francis[1]*

So, we saw another reason for this little book: before the young begin to ask for our wisdom, we need to reflect upon our rich and gifted experience! And so, we have included some of Pope Francis' gems within our book.

Spring, Summer, Autumn and Winter, as images for the stages of life, launched our process of writing the book. Gradually, two other themes came to us as ones which really focus our hope for this book: God's abiding presence with us throughout life and parables, that story form that was a favorite of Jesus. Finally, the wisdom of St. Ignatius Loyola brought into focus the roles of memory, imagination, colloquy and choice as helps for prayer about the seasons of one's life.

We recognize the profound need which a person of any age has for the reassurance that God is with us—guiding, consoling, challenging, clarifying, and companioning us in ways that give meaning and purpose to each life. Viewing one's life as a parable—a simple event flavored with surprise and challenge and mystery—invites us into a new exploration of the days and years of our life. They may have seemed ordinary and of little importance as we first experienced them. However, reflection upon the eras of our life so far, with the intent of finding God's presence and action within them, will lead us to appreciate the mystery and gift of God to us at all times and in surprising ways. It will also help us to become compassionate contemplatives, a role which has always, in one form or another, been the vocation of the elders in society.

This book, while reflecting on the experience of living and aging, is not intended as an aid to dealing with all or even any of the various "issues" that may occur as one ages. Regardless of issues, health, age, gender, family or economic circumstance, we are always called to hope and deepened gratitude for gifts we do not deserve. Our memory and imagination can open us to those gifts. While this book does not focus in a specific way upon our responsibilities for a world in need of justice, an underlying assumption is that we are always called to justice, i.e. fidelity to the responsibilities of relationships. For some, aging offers new space and time in which to give active expression to our solidarity with and compassion for a world marked by suffering of every kind. For others, aging is the time in which we can no longer evade the invitation to become a contemplative engaged in the "long, loving look at the real."[2] Gratitude and hope are key dispositions for both ways of extending the Reign of God in our midst.

Our book has been written because people have asked us to do so and because we are aware of the hunger for meaning and purpose among those who are honestly acknowledging the dynamics of aging within themselves. As co-authors, we will rejoice if deepened gratitude and hope are the fruit of prayer with this book. Our prayer is that, as you look back over your life — the events, the people, the moments to remember, — you will gradually realize all is gift — and "a joy to be shared by the whole people." Luke 2:10[3]

SUGGESTIONS
FOR USING THIS BOOK

*O*ur ways of reading books as well as our ways of praying develop over many years and as a result of many experiences. Undoubtedly, you will bring that experience to reading and using this book. And you may discover ways of using it that have not occurred to us. However, these few ideas about using the book may serve to get you started and to clarify what the book offers.

Part I: As Years Unfold: A Glance at the Journey

Part I offers a brief overview of the interior journey which many experience as we encounter the changes which aging brings—whether to us directly or to loved ones. These brief descriptions are geared to stimulating your reflection on your experience. The reflection questions can help you to own and process your own experience. This part of the book sets the stage for the explorations of your life as found in the following sections and it may be helpful to return to this section from time to time as you pray your way through the book. Above all, stop, pause and pray whenever something catches your attention! This book is especially designed to guide you as you savor and ponder your life experience quietly and prayerfully.

Part II: Ignatian Wisdom For Living

This part begins with a bit of the wisdom in the Christian story as found in the parables and conversations of Jesus. It is a simple invitation to view your own life as a living and dynamic parable and to be assured by Jesus of His desire to be in conversation with you. Reflection on experience is what Jesus did with the woman at the well, with Thomas, Peter, Martha, and the Emmaus disciples. Consequently, it is no surprise to find reflection on experience at the heart of Ignatian spirituality. Reflection on experience is Ignatian Wisdom in everyday life. Whether Jesus lived to be your age or not, he's deeply involved in your experience and wants to talk with you about it. The themes of parable and conversation are woven into the subsequent parts of the book. With these topics, as with many others, we "throw out a spray of seeds" which may find just the right soil in your desires and reflections.

God's word is unpredictable in its power. The Gospel speaks of a seed which, once sown, grows by itself, even as the farmer sleeps (Mk 4:26–29). The Church has to accept this unruly freedom of the word, which accomplishes what it wills in ways that surpass our calculations and ways of thinking.

Pope Francis[4]

This part of our book taps into the tradition of Ignatian spirituality as found in the key text of St. Ignatius of Loyola, *The Spiritual Exercises*. It draws from that tradition several key elements that offer wise suggestions for reflecting upon experience. These elements are memory, imagination, the prayer form "colloquy" and discernment or "spirit-filled choices." With each section there are reflection questions designed to encourage you to stop and reflect on how the idea finds expression in your experience. Just as Jesus invited people to reflect on their experience, this book invites you to learn from reflecting on your own rich life experiences!

This section is not intended as an extensive treatment of the Ignatian elements. Our earlier books, *Moment By Moment: A Retreat in Everyday Life* and *Finding God in Each Moment: The Practice of Discernment in Everyday Life* may be of help if you want to pursue further reflection on the elements as they appear in *The Spiritual Exercises*. For those of you who are meeting the Ignatian themes for the first time, the elements may serve by giving you language for and new understanding of some of your life experiences. For those of you who are familiar with *The Spiritual Exercises*, these reflections and those in Part III (Seasons) may stir your memories and draw upon your understanding of the themes. All of Parts I and II are intended as preparation for your journey through the Seasons of your life which is presented in Part III.

Part III: The Seasons—The Parables of Our Lives

At the beginning of Part III, the section entitled "A Mosaic for Praying with the Seasons" explains the elements of this part of the book and offers ways of praying about the Seasons of your life with Part III as a guide. It will become apparent to you as you move through this section of the book that your experience is being enhanced by what you discovered earlier in the book about the roles of memory, imagination, prayer and discernment.

Part IV: Sharing Your Story

This section contains encouragement to share your experience with others in a group. While the book has not been designed as a retreat book or conversation guide, it may serve you in those ways. Now you may be ready and want to share your reflections on your faith journey with others. This is what Mary did when she visited her cousin Elizabeth, what the Samaritan woman who met Jesus at the well shared with her neighbors, what the Emmaus disciples shared when returning to the Jerusalem community. This shared faith conversation advances the Reign of God! In a similar way, sharing your reflection upon your faith journey advances the Reign of God. Now you are one who carries the wisdom of an elder in and for this time.

PART I

AS YEARS UNFOLD:
A Glance at the Journey

Reflection

*N*ow, in this moment, it can be helpful to step back from the daily scrutiny of our lives to ponder the big picture—the broad expanse of experience which is unfolding. No matter which birthday we—or our loved ones—just celebrated, or how our days appear to us, reflection on our life experiences is an important aspect of aging well and gracefully. It is a help to accepting the repeated challenges which the unfolding years of our lives hold because we begin to recognize in them the providential care of a loving God. This little book offers you a way to ponder the big picture, to wonder at the unfolding mystery of your aging. It offers another frame for viewing your life experience. It doesn't ask you "to do something about it" as much as to allow yourself to discover and name your current place in the process of aging. It may also allow you to marvel at the way you have moved through earlier stages and to grow in trust that God has been at work in your experience.

While memories of regrets and glitches in the journey may come to light, the invitation may be to view them now within the broad perspective of your entire life. With that awareness and honest acceptance of "where one is," you can respond to God's daily call with new fidelity.

Days are rhythmic. When we are centered, we can notice the rhythms and even the patterns which form the rhythms. What Saint Ignatius of Loyola teaches us about the structure of a prayer period can also give us insight about the unfolding of the days, the weeks, even the seasons that make up our lives.

✦ Awareness of desire and longing come at the beginning of the time of prayer.

✦ Reflection and conscious awareness of oneself and God grow as the prayer time unfolds.

✦ Gratitude, wonder and awe before the steady gifts of God mark the final part of that prayer time.

✦ The action of God and our response in prayer also plant seeds of hope for what the next day, week, season, the future will hold for us.

Desire, longing, reflection, conscious awareness, gratitude, wonder, awe, and hope: these elements mark the development of a Christian life as well as a period of prayer. They are also the spiritual dynamics at work when we experience and respond to the parables that form our particular life. We try to listen and to see God's mysterious action even in the puzzling aspects of our lives. We may struggle with the challenge which our life parable carries. Gradually, joyful gratitude and peaceful hope signal the presence within of the Spirit who acts in us as She prays in us. We are made ready to be a new and refreshing parable in our place in the world.

In Part I, we offer an overview of the journey of aging with lots of space in which to find your current place. It is not meant to be a sociological or psychological analysis of the aging process. Rather, it offers simple, brief descriptions of the interior awareness that grows as the stages of aging unfold. It suggests that the stages unfold not without meaning and purpose, but as part of one's life-long vocation. It offers a context for discovering and naming where you currently dwell within the reality of aging as an on-going process led by God. Some words help to "name the place," allowing you to befriend your experience, to become more accepting of it. The inclusion of parables is a reminder that our lives as parables also carry the imprint of mystery and surprise at every stage. Our attitude towards our aging experience is so critically important. Sprinkled throughout Part I and the book are poems reflecting on the reality and mystery of aging. Hopefully, these poems will affirm your experience of aging and encourage a life-giving attitude within you.

PART I As Years Unfold

"As Years Unfold" not only helps you to name where you are, but it also invites you to begin the process of deepening your gratitude for how God has been present and active in blessing you in earlier stages of your aging. As that gratitude is nurtured, it can yield a quiet hope and confidence that your life will continue to unfold within the providential ways of God. Responding to God's on-going call becomes a reason for your days' efforts and actions. You might want to return to Part I from time to time as a reminder to trust that our lives unfold within the loving presence of the God of all seasons. We have wonderful reasons for gratitude and hope! Our lives are filled with moments to remember!

Each paragraph in this chapter attempts to capture in broad themes a stage through which most people seem to progress as we move through the later years of our lives. The paragraphs are presented in a sequence which seems to ring true to the aging process as it unfolds in most people. At the same time, we recognize that it might be more true to life to describe the experience as circles and loops since we may revisit some of the experiences more than once in our journey. You may find yourself revisiting a description more than once. While we have tried to be inclusive and respectful of the gender differences within the experience of men and women, you may want to include your own additions to give a fuller picture of the richness of your own personal life journey.

To support reflection and prayer as one looks for and embraces the stage "where we are," we offer a scripture passage that affirms the experience as well as a few reflection questions to begin your appreciation and appropriation of the experience. It is not surprising to find a bit of resistance within as we begin to acknowledge that we are aging. Hopefully, praying with this section—in your own way, your own time and at your own pace—will serve to confirm your contemplative wonder and gratitude before the providential presence and action of God throughout your lifetime. Such wonder and gratitude can ground our hope for the future, a hope to be fulfilled only when we see God as God really is.

"Grow old along with me! The best is yet to be."

Robert Browning[5]

Owning the Transition

No one after lighting a lamp hides it under a jar, or puts it under a bed, but puts it on a lampstand, so that those who enter may see the light. For nothing is hidden that will not be disclosed, nor is anything secret that will not become known and come to light. Then pay attention to how you listen…hear the word of God and do it.

Parable of the Lamp, Luke 8:16–21

In your old age, I shall be still the same; when your hair is grey, I shall still support you. I have already done so, I have carried you, I shall still support and deliver you.

Isaiah 46:47

There is a season for everything, a time for every occupation under heaven.

Ecclesiastes 3:18

A day dawns when we become aware that we are aging—moving beyond the years marked by career goals, family plans, relationship-building, inquiry and investigation. Aging's identity for us isn't quite clear. There have been signals all along the way. Many things can heighten our awareness—visits to doctors, receiving mail from AARP, a few more gray hairs, the birth of a grandchild—and we may dance around the reality for a while.

The awareness of our aging may not be a "downer" and it may not sadden us at all. Our awakening to this new time in our life may come in the form of a new opportunity. Youth, middle age and senior years have traditionally been numerically determined and various cultures have markers for "retirement" ages. However, we all know people whose "young at heart and full of life" spirit belies the date on their birth certificate and spurs them on in a new venture. Even new opportunities, such as long distance travel or taking a Spanish course or some service at the local food pantry, can open new worlds to us and deepen our gratitude for our life experience. We recognize the wisdom of "planning for the future" as we wonder and muse about "what will I do when I retire?"

Finally we can begin to call it "home" though it surely is not a place that allows "settling in." Something *is* changing! As with all other stages in our lives, it carries with it an invitation from God that may only gradually become clear. It is to God that we make our daily response. From there the mysterious life process unfolds and presses us to a new consciousness of who we are before the God who has loved us faithfully all along the way.

◊ What awakened you to this new experience in your life?

◊ What seems to be God's invitation to you now?

◊ What challenges you and what encourages you to embrace your life now?

Prayer

by Patrick Purnell, SJ[6]

(For Liz)

Prayer is by nature elusive.
You can put all the pieces together
Ready yourself
As you would to welcome a guest
"Delighted you could come!"
And the guest fades away on the door-step.
You're mistaken!
There was no guest. It was but a mirage.
You run through the process once more,
Making sure you've left nothing out.
And you are left with the tea and the cakes.
Where are you? I long for you to come.
Why are you so difficult to find?
Is there some secret I am not privy to?
Do you give the key to but a privileged few?
I sit and wait like the lone dawn bird
For the first rays of your sun.
Knowing that you are not to be sought for or found.
For you are the seeking
You are the finding.

Collecting What Has Been

Again, the kingdom of heaven is like a net that was thrown into the sea and caught fish of every kind; when it was full, they drew it ashore, sat down, and put the good into baskets but threw out the bad.

Parable of the Net, Matthew 13:47

*I*nitially the awareness of aging may bother us—or others who love us—and we may seem to be looking backward and longing for what was. Taking that turn of attention seriously can lead us to recall and remember the particulars of our life: the people, places, decisions, events, the moments of pain and confusion, of exultation and harmony. It may also awaken us to what we still want to do, who we still want to become. It may become a time of healing or reordering of our priorities. We may realize that others do treasure us and our contribution—even as it changes. As with a precious jewel, we turn the experience around over and over; finally, we notice and surrender to God's mysterious action for our great good within it. That loving mercy of God in our lives that brought us to this moment frees us for new discoveries.

◊ What helps you to entertain this new possibility of aging, and perhaps gradually to "own" it as your place in the world now?

◊ Who in your life helps you honestly to deal with this reality?

◊ Where do you find the tools to balance the apparently disparate parts of the experience?

◊ Do you have a personal Wisdom figure whose inspiration steadies you?

Holy Ground
by Irene Zimmerman[7]

(Exodus 3:1–5)

I went to the desert one morning
and walked with Moses in the sand
to where the bush was burning.
That it did not turn to ash
was no surprise to me
for so I'd seen it burning
throughout my childhood days.

But suddenly a voice called out to me
from that bush!
Moses left.
Take off your shoes, I heard,
for the life on which you stand is holy.
I am the ONE WHO IS
and this is how I hold you.

I stood barefoot on the ground
of my life history,
burning through and through
with that mystery.

Gratitude

I thank my God every time I remember you, constantly praying with joy in every one of my prayers for all of you.... I am confident that the one who began a good work among you will bring it to completion by the day of Jesus Christ. It is right for me to think this way about all of you, because you hold me in your heart....how I long for all of you with the compassion of Christ Jesus. And this is my prayer, that your love may overflow more and more with knowledge and full insight to help you to determine what is best....

Philippians 1:3, 4, 7–9

Saying "thank you" may have been part of one's life since childhood, but it has a deeper, more luminous quality to it now. As we ponder *Moments to Remember*, we continually grow in our awareness and appreciation that all is gift. The talents, the people, the circumstances and opportunities, the struggles and accomplishments, and so much more are reasons to pause and to ponder the generosity of God. There is much in a life that surprises us. Change has already happened in so many ways. Unresolved questions may beg again for our new answers, answers enriched by our own maturity. It may take more time than we thought it would to become grateful. While we may still prefer to be the givers, we find that we say "thank you" more often and more easily. We appreciate in a new way that "all is gift." Gradually, gratitude becomes the foundation from which we move into the future with hope.

PART I As Years Unfold

◊ What are your customary ways of thanking God and other people?

◊ How has your appreciation of Eucharist grown during your lifetime?

◊ What recent experiences or events have led you to deeper gratitude?

You loved us first
by Soren Kierkegaard[8]

...You loved us first, oh God. Alas we speak of it as if you loved us first one time only, ...when in very truth, without ceasing, you love us first all the time. When I awaken in the morning and my soul turns at once toward you, you are first. You have already turned toward me. If I rise at dawn and in the very first second of my awakening my soul turns to you in prayer, you have beat me to it. You have already turned in love toward me. Thus we speak ingratitude if, unthankful and unaware, we speak of you as having loved us first only one time.

Learning to Wait for the Spirit to Lead

Likewise the Spirit helps us in our weakness; for we do not know how to pray as we ought, but that very Spirit intercedes with sighs too deep for words. And God, who searches the heart, knows what is the mind of the Spirit, because the Spirit intercedes for the saints according to the will of God.

Romans 8:26–27

*T*races of our dreaming about the future may appear in many forms: travel brochures, flight costs, retirement planning details, health care provisions, real estate facts, books to be read, golf courses, details of curiosity to be pursued, a "bucket list." Or we may just find ourselves savoring the gift of time. With the gift of health and perhaps enough money to pay the bills, we may be "ready to go." And then the strange phenomenon of delay, obstacles, new opportunities, doubts and wonderings, happy or stunning surprises become one's daily companion.

Gradually, we are made aware once again of the role of waiting in our lives. In our haste to move forward and not get trapped by living in the past or looking back, we can forget the role of the Spirit who leads and draws us into the future in the world of human affairs. With a new consciousness of the insistent ways of the Spirit, we reset our interior GPS and find more peace.

◊ How do you want to focus your attention and energies now?

◊ Does it seem realistic to be able to focus in those ways?

◊ How are you more aware of the daily inspiration of the Spirit?

Trust in the slow work of God
by Pierre Teilhard de Chardin, SJ[9]

Above all, trust in the slow work of God.

We are quite naturally impatient in everything
    to reach the end without delay.
    We should like to skip the intermediate stages.
    We are impatient of being on the way to
    something
    unknown, something new.

And yet it is the law of progress
    that it is made by passing through
    some states of instability—
    and that it may take a very long time.

And so I think it is with you.
    Your ideas mature gradually—let them grow,
    let them shape themselves, without undue haste.

Don't try to force them on,
    as though you could be today what time
    (that is to say, grace and circumstances
    acting on your own good will)
    will make of you tomorrow.

Only God could say what this new spirit
    gradually forming within you will be.
    Give Our Lord the benefit of believing
    that his hand is leading you,

and accept the anxiety of feeling yourself
    in suspense and incomplete.

Moments to Remember

Longing and Wishing
that Things were Different

I do not understand my own actions. For I do not do what I want, but I do the very thing I hate….I can will what is right, but I cannot do it. For I do not do the good I want, but the evil I do not want is what I do….So I find it to be a law that when I want to do what is good, evil lies close at hand….Wretched man that I am! Who will rescue me…? Thanks be to God through Jesus Christ our Lord!

Romans 7:15, 18–19, 21, 24–25

*A*lmost in inverse proportion to the freeing action of the Spirit, another inner feeling can assert itself. Its tell-tale signs are boredom, lack of interest, doubt, irritation, a critic's voice, a flash of intense feeling, a type of dumbing down. "If only" echoes within and gradually awakens us to longings and desires that may be nebulous, but are concrete enough to signal that even at this age of life, we are able to try to be the "sovereign planner" of our lives. We may notice that we are arguing with facts, with national and international news, with spunky grandchildren. We may struggle with the delusion that we are always right. We may need a walk through the neighborhood or a drive around the lake or a leisurely cup of tea to help us find our spot on the map again. It may humble us and return us to gratitude for the merciful planning of God who knows of what we are made. Then we are ready to make new efforts to attend to the Spirit's movements within and around us.

PART I As Years Unfold

◊ What do you wish were different in your life now?

◊ Is it somehow connected to similar patterns from earlier in your life?

◊ Have you thought about your God-given vocation recently?

The Homemaker God

by Irene Zimmerman[10]

(Luke 15:8–10)

The Homemaker God has come to my house
to search for the lost coin of me
which I, in my miserly morning,
thinking this frugal and wise
and worthy of praise and grace,
had in a safe "good place."

The Homemaker God has taken her broom
and swept from attic to basement,
moved cupboards and dressers,
stripped beds, emptied drawers—
now she's checking each pantry shelf
for the silver coins of myself.

The Homemaker God will find me, I trust—
she knows how to raise dust.

Reality Factors

As he approached Jericho, a blind man was sitting by the roadside begging. When he heard a crowd going by, he asked what was happening. They told him, "Jesus of Nazareth is passing by." Then he shouted, "Jesus, Son of David, have mercy on me!" Those who were in front sternly ordered him to be quiet; but he shouted even more loudly, "Son of David, have mercy on me!" Jesus stood still and ordered the man to be brought to him; and when he came near, he asked him, "What do you want me to do for you?" He said, "Lord, let me see again." Jesus said to him, "Receive your sight; your faith has saved you." Immediately he regained his sight and followed him, glorifying God; and all the people, when they saw it, praised God.

Luke 18:35–43

So often, a quick quip about "reality" will have a barb in it. It forgets that the Incarnation, God-With-Us, has the particularity of the real about it. Attending to God's presence and action as we age will surely mean watching scores: those that record our health or the gyrations of a financial world and those that signal a favorite team's plight or delight. Other particulars also get our attention: noticing the small kindness that seems to open a door, the call from a grandchild, the newspaper clipping sent by an old friend. Each mysteriously makes us more aware of God's presence to us and our need of God. There is a growing comfort and peace in being "known" and loved by God. Limits that present themselves suddenly or gradually, events that may carry harshness or gentleness, and reminders of unfinished business invite us to that same consciousness of God's faithful presence and action and our constant need of God. A lifetime of praying over the life of Jesus reminds us that Gospel themes are carried in all events. We ask that we may see.

◊ What do you see now? What "sight" do you need to accept?

◊ Where and upon whom do you place your focus?

◊ What is your favorite prayer when you are in need?

Known

by Charles K. Robinson[11]

I know you, I created you. I am creating you. I have
loved you from your mother's womb.

You have fled—as you now know—from my love. But I
love you nevertheless, and not-the-less, however far you
flee, it is I who sustain your very power of fleeing, and I
will never finally let you go.

I accept you as you are. You are forgiven.

I know all your sufferings. I have always known them.
For beyond your understanding, when you suffer, I suffer.

I also know all the little tricks by which you try to hide
the ugliness you have made of your life, from yourself
and others.

But you are beautiful.

You are beautiful more deeply within than you know.

You are beautiful because you yourself in the unique
one that only you are, reflect already something of the
beauty of my holiness

in a way which shall never end.

You are beautiful also because I, and I alone, see the
beauty you shall become.

Through the transforming power of my love you shall
become perfectly beautiful. You shall become perfectly
beautiful in a uniquely irreplaceable way,

which neither you nor I will work out alone,

for we shall work it out together.

Possibility of Newness

When a woman is in labor, she has pain, because her hour has come. But when her child is born, she no longer remembers the anguish because of the joy of having brought a human being into the world. So you have pain now; but I will see you again, and your hearts will rejoice, and no one will take your joy from you. When that day comes, you will not ask me any questions.

John 16:21–23

*J*ust when we think we have "seen it all," recognized and known how Jesus would act in our lives and invite us to follow Him, a new gesture of God becomes apparent to us. It may require some time, some conversation, and some reflection before we recognize that the invitation is from God. We respond in ways that are characteristic of us, have always been "just like us," but with a new twist, dimension, degree, determination. We may notice a new readiness in us. And something else dawns upon us. We recognize now that our road is filled with many travelers all heading Home. We are not alone, but we really are members of a community of delightful folks. In that companionship and with the help of others on the journey, it is easier to detect the voice of the Spirit and to take up the Spirit's ways of wisdom, counsel, knowledge, understanding, piety, fortitude and fear of the Lord.

◊ What new companions for the journey have you discovered?

◊ What do you find delightful about people?

◊ What are you able to contribute to this gathering of very human folks?

The Joy of the Gospel

by *Pope Francis*[12]

I invite all Christians, everywhere, at this very moment, to a renewed personal encounter with Jesus Christ, or at least an openness to letting him encounter them; I ask all of you to do this unfailingly each day. No one should think that this invitation is not meant for him or her, since "no one is excluded from the joy brought by the Lord." The Lord does not disappoint those who take this risk; whenever we take a step towards Jesus, we come to realize that he is already there, waiting for us with open arms....With a tenderness which never disappoints, but is always capable of restoring our joy, he makes it possible for us to lift up our heads and to start anew. Let us not flee from the resurrection of Jesus, let us never give up, come what will. May nothing inspire more than his life, which impels us onwards!

PART I As Years Unfold

Embracing the Ordinary
as My Place in the World

I want to know Christ and the power of his resurrection and the sharing of his sufferings by becoming like him....Not that I have already obtained this or have already reached the goal; but I press on to make it my own, because Christ Jesus has made me his own.

Philippians 3:10–12

"No problem" has found its way into our vocabulary. We have discovered that the graced response in life often takes the form of a simple and ordinary gesture, one that our life context makes possible. That insight may shed light on what has been happening throughout our lives even as we tried to match another's apparently extraordinary activity. In what is ordinary for us in our daily context, there is always the choice to allow God to act within the experience or to resist that Divine impulse. Our days are different, but the same as we *"act justly, love tenderly, and walk humbly with God"* (Micah 6:8) in our place in the world. We may be startled by the simplicity and ordinariness of each day. Our growing desire to be aware of God's presence and action may reveal the marvel and wonder buried in the simplest person, experience, and event. Flowers delight by their beauty in a new way; birds do more than just wake us in the morning; sunsets captivate us.

◊ What ordinary things give you pleasure now?

◊ Recall a recent experience that brought laughter and joy to your heart. Does laughter come more easily to you?

◊ What part of your daily routine seems especially filled with God's presence?

I am a little church

by e.e. cummings[13]

i am a little church(no great cathedral)
  far from the splendor and squalor of hurrying cities
  -i do not worry if briefer days grow briefest,
  i am not sorry when sun and rain make april

my life is the life of the reaper and the sower;
  my prayers are prayers of earth's own clumsily striving
  (finding and losing and laughing and crying)children
  whose any sadness or joy is my grief or my gladness

around me surges a miracle of unceasing
  birth and glory and death and resurrection:
  over my sleeping self float flaming symbols
  of hope, and i wake to a perfect patience of mountains

i am a little church(far from the frantic
  world with its rapture and anguish)at peace with nature
  -i do not worry if longer nights grow longest;
  i am not sorry when silence becomes singing

winter by spring, i lift my diminutive spire to
  merciful Him Whose only now is forever:
  standing erect in the deathless truth of His presence
  (welcoming humbly His light and proudly His darkness)

Transformation of Self

…it is no longer I who live, but it is Christ who lives in me. And the life I now live in the flesh I live by faith in the Son of God, who loved me and gave himself for me.

Galatians 2:20

*I*nterior peace has always been a significant indicator of our being who and where God has called us to be. It continues to be a gentle guide, but with a new fullness to it. It seems to co-exist with new anguish over experiences that carry the mysteries of suffering and evil and every kind of human frailty. Again and again we imagine how God sees the world and humanity now. We may be moved to pray and to act in some way to counter the sinfulness within and around us, but we do so with a deeper awareness of the dependence of all upon the gratuitous mercy of God. Out of the haze that may seem to blur our vision, a new consciousness emerges of who God has always called us to be. As always before in our lives, that consciousness both consoles and challenges us. Jesus' words make more sense and often seem to be just what we need to hear on a given day. And there is a new confidence that God will give us what we need to be the person we are called to be at this time in our life. We wait with more patience, united perhaps with the many around the globe who wait for food and water and shelter.

◊ What new ways of living each day are you now experiencing?

◊ How is your attention being redirected to God's activity in your life?

◊ What characterizes your prayer and concern for others, for the world?

Feelings

by Patrick Purnell, SJ[14]

'Follow!' Follow the voice that is calling:
Pick up the echoes from the valley side;
Stir memories of graces once given;
Touch the place where you last knew the way,
But were filled with the darkness of doubt;
Listen to the stirrings within you;
See the movement of shadow and light;
Recoil from the fears that beset you;
Treasure the truth deep within.
Will you stay in the boat protected securely
By rules and commandments traditionally preached,
Safe when the scales are balanced at judging,
Sure of a place with the just?
Or will you trust yourself to the pull of your feelings
And walk on the waves of the sea,
Not knowing if it's Christ who calls?
Will you risk all for fullness and freedom,
With only the white stick of love for your guide,
When you're blown by the wind, the sea and the tide,
Because you are sure you've heard a 'Come'
From the voice of the one who once bid you his 'Peace'?
And you take to the waters and dance
In the storm by the light of his face.

The Real Questions

"The words that I have spoken to you are spirit and life. But among you there are some who do not believe." For Jesus knew from the first who were the ones that did not believe, and who was the one that would betray him. Because of this many of his disciples turned back and no longer went about with him. So Jesus asked the twelve, "Do you also wish to go away?" Simon Peter answered him, "Lord, to whom can we go? You have the words of eternal life. We have come to believe and know that you are the Holy One of God."

John 6:63–69

Then, perhaps with a bang that startles us, questions stir within us. They come by day and by night, when alone and with others, in the midst of humdrum activity and in the midst of glorious celebrations. They may be stark and they are our unique articulations of the timeless questions of philosophers, poets and theologians and little children. Why? When? How? Who are You? Will You recognize me in the crowd? Is Jesus truly the Way, the Life and the Truth? Will You help me understand? What will the balance sheet look like to You? Can I live on—somehow, somewhere? And there will be other questions that surface out of each person's mind, heart and history. Once again, memories that seek still more healing and reconciliation may surface within us. Questions have a capacity to stir us up. Often the questions are answerable only with faith and hope. They can take what seems like the shortest route and send us in circles. And they can lead us to silence and awe and deeper faith, hope and love. At this part of our lives, we may have some very pointed questions to ask Jesus. And we trust we will be given what we need to embrace the answer.

◊ What are your questions now? Do they resemble ones of an earlier time in your life? Have they been triggered by a memory that needs healing?

◊ What helps you to hold the unanswerable questions with peace?

◊ Is there a question you would love to have answered by God today?

Letter 4

in *Letters to a Young Poet*
by Rainer Maria Rilke[15]

I want to beg you, as much as I can, dear sir, to be patient toward all that is unsolved in your heart and to try to love the *questions themselves* like locked rooms and like books that are written in a very foreign tongue. Do not now search the answers, which cannot be given to you because you would not be able to live them. And the point is, to live everything. *Live* the questions now. Perhaps you will then gradually, without noticing it, live along some distant day into the answer....

I would like to beg you, dear Sir, as well as I can, to have patience with everything unresolved in your heart and to try to love the questions themselves as if they were locked rooms or books written in a very foreign language. Don't search for the answers, which could not be given to you now, because you would not be able to live them. And the point is, to live everything. Live the questions now. Perhaps then, someday far in the future, you will gradually, without even noticing it, live your way into the answer.

In God's Time and in God's Own Way

There are others who are slow and need help, who lack strength and abound in poverty; but the eyes of the Lord look kindly upon them; he lifts them out of their lowly condition and raises up their heads to the amazement of the many. Good things and bad, life and death, poverty and wealth, come from the Lord. The Lord's gift remains with the devout, and his favor brings lasting success.... Stand by your agreement and attend to it, and grow old in your work. Do not wonder at the works of a sinner, but trust in the Lord and keep at your job; for it is easy in the sight of the Lord to make the poor rich suddenly, in an instant.

Sirach 11:12–17, 20–21

The process of aging seems to have a hidden trajectory at work in it. Again and again, we are brought to the awareness in our whole being of "in God's time and in God's own way." More and more we recognize that the right time, place, circumstance, persons, sequence of events seems to be "in God's time and in God's own way." God seems to be more than a traveling companion on this life journey. Providential Planner might better capture our sense of God's abiding presence to us. As we reminisce about the times when we thought we were planner/doer-in-chief, we might be humbled to say: *"Didn't our hearts burn within us as He spoke to us on the way?"*

◊ Where do you see God's time and God's way at work?

◊ What reassurance or discomfort does that divine action stir in you?

◊ Are you more ready to allow God to guide you in your life?

For surely I know the plans I have for you, says the Lord, plans for your welfare and not for harm, to give you a future with hope. Then when you call upon me and come and pray to me, I will hear you. When you search for me, you will find me; if you seek me with all your heart, I will let you find me, says the Lord, and I will restore your fortunes and gather you from all the nations and all the places where I have driven you, says the Lord, and I will bring you back to the place from which I sent you into exile.

Jeremiah 29:11–14

PART I As Years Unfold

A New Person with a New Vision

In this you rejoice, even if now for a little while you have had to suffer various trials, so that the genuineness of your faith—being more precious than gold that, though perishable, is tested by fire—may be found to result in praise and glory and honor when Jesus Christ is revealed. Although you have not seen him, you love him; and even though you do not see him now, you believe in him and rejoice with an indescribable and glorious joy, for you are receiving the outcome of your faith, the salvation of your souls.

1 Peter 1:6–9

Now I know only in part; then I will know fully, even as I have been fully known.

1 Corinthians 13:12

*O*ur fascination with the saints and with famous women and men of prior times may be because they have somehow captured and shared a glimpse of the vision that guides us all on the journey. But it is our turn now. It is our turn to live grounded in our truest identity and to pursue the vision of life that has coherence and meaning for us. Whether others grasp who we are becoming has little, or less, importance to us. Even as it may separate us a bit from the whirling crowds, the person we are becoming may be part of

God's drawing others more deeply into the mystery of life. Our life may provoke new moments to remember in their lives. Our life may indeed be a parable. Without intending it, we may model for others a way of aging that frees the Spirit to work in the world. We are grateful in that hope. We look forward to God telling us the story of our life as it has unfolded before God.

◊ What do you hope to say to God when you meet God?

◊ What do you imagine God will say to you when you meet?

◊ Would Jesus' mother Mary be a good companion for you now?

What you hold, may you always hold

by Clare of Assisi[16]

…What you hold, may you always hold,
what you do, may you keep doing and not stop,
but with swift pace, nimble step, and feet that
do not stumble so that even your walking does
not raise any dust,
may you go forward tranquilly, joyfully, briskly
and cautiously along the path of happiness,
trusting in no one and agreeing with no one
because he might want to dissuade you from
pursuing your founding purpose or might place
a stumbling block in your way,
preventing you, in that perfection with which
the Spirit of the Lord has called you, from fulfilling
your vows to the Most High….

PART II

IGNATIAN WISDOM FOR LIVING

Remembering and Imagining

God's love shines down upon me like the light rays from the sun, or God's love is poured forth lavishly like a fountain spilling forth its waters into an unending stream. Just as I see the sun in its rays and the fountain in its waters, so God pours forth a sharing in divine life in all the gifts showered upon me. God's delight and joy is to be with the ones called God's children — to be with me. God cannot do enough to speak out and show love for me — ever calling and inviting me to a fuller and better life, a sharing in divine life.

Sp. Ex. 237[17]

*M*emory and Imagination are precious gifts from God and they enrich our lives. They are a primary place for the action of the Holy Spirit. Ignatius of Loyola placed great importance on "remembering" and "imagining." They serve as the basis for many prayer experiences in his classic text, *The Spiritual Exercises.* His early companions begged him on several occasions to "remember" the significant "moments" or "core faith experiences" in his life. Reluctantly, he began to share the memories with Fr. Luis Gonzalez de Camara. His "remembering" became his *Autobiography,* a rich text in our Christian spiritual tradition and one that guided later generations in their decisions. We might have a similar experience when grandchildren or younger friends ask us to tell them about periods of our life. Recalling the action of God and human response is a great way to learn and to discover what is important in life!

◊ What memories are important to you now?

◊ How aware are you of your imagination at work?

◊ What new understanding of your memories and imagination occurs to you when you think of them as a place in which God continues to act in your life now?

Remembering

*O*ur lives are filled with moments to remember. "Remembering" allows us to reflect on our experience with God and other people. "Remembering" can be a way of praying whereby we use our memory to remember God's loving action and presence in us and in our lives. In wisdom and because of his practical experience, Ignatius encouraged the use of "memory, understanding and will." This way of praying is a help to becoming more free when one is pondering important issues, realities or decisions.

> The structure of these exercises has the purpose of leading a person to a true spiritual freedom. We grow into this freedom by gradually bringing an order of values into our lives so that we find that at the moment of choice or decision we are not swayed by any disordered love.
>
> *Sp. Ex. 21*[18]

◊ Select a favorite memory and ponder how it helps you to approach life with a free spirit.

◊ Select a painful memory to bring to prayer. As you pray about it, ask God to help you to hold that memory with more freedom.

◊ What current choices are being affected by your memories? Can you grow in more freedom in those areas of choice?

◊ Pause to remember persons with whom sharing memories has been life giving.

◊ Pause to remember a moment in your life when revisiting a retreat journal or diary or discovering old family pictures you were flooded with feelings of gratitude—moments to remember!

Imagining

> I beg for the gift of an intimate knowledge of all the goods which God lovingly shares with me. Filled with gratitude, I want to be empowered to respond just as totally in my love and service.
>
> *Sp. Ex. 233*[19]

*I*n a child's world, everything is new. Their imaginations are free to create, discover and "make believe." These "play-time-games" become new experiences and fresh memories and fill their lives, and ours, with wonder. The history of art and literature demonstrates how hungry our imaginations have been. Architecture, too, has nourished our imaginations. Cathedrals and stained glass windows have stirred our imaginations and filled our memories with themes of scripture and the endless human search for God.

In our technological era, some may have become more dependent upon TV, ebooks, internet and cinema to supply food for imagination, leading some to fear technology's impact upon the imagination. However, experience is demonstrating that the possibilities offered by technology also stir creativity and imagination.

◊ How has the creative imagination of artists, poets, musicians enriched your life?

◊ What aspects of technology delight you? Bother you? Frighten you?

◊ As you recall your personal history, what developments in technology have played a role?

◊ What helps you to blend the arts and technology in ways that enrich you and others?

◊ In your life, who inspires and ignites your imagination?

Wisdom reminds us that we need to be discerning about the use of technology, using it in so far as it helps us—and others—to be the women and men in whom God takes delight. Ignatius offered some of that wisdom within the grounding statement for all the spiritual exercises, the "Principle and Foundation." David Fleming, SJ captures that wisdom in these words:

God who loves us creates us and wants to share life with us forever. Our love response takes shape in our praise and honor and service of the God of our life. All the things in this world are also created because of God's love and they become a context of gifts, presented to us so that we can know God more easily and make a return of love more readily. As a result, we show reverence for all the gifts of creation....But if we abuse any...or take them as the center of our lives, we break our relationship with God and hinder our growth as loving persons....we must hold ourselves in balance....Our only desire and our one choice should be this: I want and I choose what better leads to God's deepening life in me.

Sp. Ex. 23[20]

◊ What happens when you pray to view all in your life — people, events, places, circumstances — as gifts?

◊ In what areas of your life are you being invited to a better balance?

◊ As you make your way through this period of your life, what seems to be God's invitation "to let go and let God?"

Our imagination might play with options that "might have been" and, in that, the Spirit might be inviting us to surrender dreams of the past and to ponder with new gratitude the loving providence of God in our lives. The Spirit may add energy to our imaginings of a good idea. It may be our imaginations which help us to discover new ways of serving others as we age. Our imagination may suggest new ways of arranging ordinary details — sitting in a different place at a meeting, planning an impromptu party, adding spice to a recipe or rearranging things in the garage. The Ignatian principle of reflection on experience can guide us as we open to the action of the Spirit in our memories and imaginings.

◊ What is now apparent to you as places in your daily routine where your imagination is at work?

◊ Make some time to notice the way the Spirit adds energy to many—but perhaps not all—of your "good ideas."

◊ When it becomes apparent that an idea or plan won't be possible, ask God for the gift of surrendering to God's ways which can be made known to us in so many other ways.

A Blend of Memory and Imagination

*T*he "Principle and Foundation" quoted above may also be a helpful guide to us when we consider memories of the past or dreams and images of the future. It can help us frame the questions or choices before us:

◊ When you ponder these memories or imaginings now, do they lead and help you to be more the person God calls you to be?

◊ Is there movement forward in your awareness and gratitude or in your sorrow and repentance?

◊ Or do any memories or imaginings focus you in another direction such as worry or discouragement?

The answers to those questions can guide us to choices about entertaining the memories and imaginings which will lead us to peace and gratitude, rather than those that turn us to worry about the past or anxiety about the future. Above all, we will learn to place our lives — past, present and future — into God's hands.

While aging is notorious for compromising our ability to remember persons, names, events, we may find ingenious ways of addressing daily challenges. They may surprise even us! It may at times be a struggle to be open to God's word at work in those memories. Almost paradoxically, even as we begin to cherish our most precious memories, we may also be stunned by some painful memories. We may even fear what will emerge from memories of the past. In the light of God's providence and with Jesus as companion, we may gain a different perspective on an event so that regret, too, may yield to gratitude and wonder at God's wisdom.

"Stop day-dreaming and get back to work" may have been a phrase that countered the use of imagination and memory earlier in our lives. It may require some gentle encouragement for us to engage in the rich world of memory and imagination. The Spirit offers that encouragement to us, probably on a daily basis. It comes in the memory flash of a face from long ago, or the lyrics of a song that summon details of an event long forgotten, but deeply formative of our faith. Always the life, death and resurrection of Jesus serve as the pattern for our lives too! Clearly, our gifts of memory and imagination carry God's word to us. There may still be more that God will reveal to us now as we pray with these gifts.

God's invitation will be to deepened gratitude for what has been and confident hope in God's presence to us as we move along in life. At times, the invitation may be to healing of a memory or the acceptance of the consequences of a decision. We may be invited to surrender some of our dreams as well as our past disappointments. Wise friends can support us as we bring into the light of conversation the new awareness.

Jesus always offers a listening ear to our memories and stories. Jesus' story continually offers us new perspective on our lives. God's imagination is without limit in offering us the beauty of creation and the marvels of humanity. God's endless fidelity to us demonstrates God's good memory and rich imagination.

"Prayer for me is always a prayer full of memory, of recollection, even the memory of my own history or what the Lord has done…. But above all, I also know that the Lord remembers me. I can forget about him, but I know that he never, ever forgets me."

Pope Francis.[21]

Suggestion for Prayer

*A*s a way of becoming attentive to the Spirit's encouragement in your remembering and imagining, you might wish to use a simple adaptation of the examen of consciousness, an important form of Ignatian prayer:

✦ Begin each day with your own prayer to the Spirit, asking to be open and attentive to the action of the Spirit in your memory and imagination.

✦ End each day with your prayer of gratitude to the Spirit for her action in your life that day.

✦ Consider sharing some of your memories or imaginings with a wise friend who can remind you of God's activity if you forget that step.

✦ If, in the past, practices such as journaling or writing letters or sketching images have been ways of clarifying your experience or expressing yourself, plan some time in your week or day in which you can do that again.

◊ After that practice, what has become more evident to you?

◊ How can you incorporate that awareness into your daily life and prayer?

◊ How do you need the Spirit's comfort or inspiration now?

THE PRESENT MOMENT
by Lenora Benda, CSJ[22]

I hold in my hands this moment — the now,
then another moment — and another.
I become aware of each one...
— each one to treasure, to hold, to be aware of.
It will never come again — the now,
for it changes and becomes another now.
Hold it, treasure it, be present to it, be aware of it.

This is the moment...
Ponder, take a deep breath, feel the air, look around.
This same moment will be gone in a moment,
only to allow another to come.

This is the moment: don't miss it, don't forget it,
hold it in your heart.
It will never be repeated exactly the same
be ready, accept the next one.

Know that God is there; God is here. He is present...
be aware, believe, trust, treasure
THE PRESENT MOMENT. It is Jesus !

Colloquy:
A Conversation In Prayer

Now during those days he went out to the mountain to pray; and he spent the night in prayer to God.

Luke 6:12

At that time Jesus said, "I thank you, Father, Lord of heaven and earth, because you have hidden these things from the wise and the intelligent and have revealed them to infants; yes, Father, for such was your gracious will."

Matthew 11:25–26

God gifts me with the fullness of divine life in Jesus. God's only Son is not only the Word in whom all things are created, but also the Word who becomes flesh and dwells with us....God loves me so much that I become a dwelling-place or temple of God—growing in an ever-deepening realization of the image and likeness of God which is the glory shining out of human creation.

Sp. Ex. 235[23]

The Conversations of Jesus

*J*esus is a wise friend who is always ready for a good conversation with us! One type of intimate conversation in prayer is the prayer-form of "Colloquy," an important dimension of the contemplative prayer developed by Ignatius in *The Spiritual Exercises*. It is very simply described as a prayer of intimate conversation usually, but not necessarily, with Jesus at the end of a time of prayer. When we ponder the conversations of Jesus, we discover Jesus is a wonderful teacher. In his life, Jesus used example, parables and questions. Jesus also taught us by his way of engaging in conversation with others. The behavior of both the apostles and the disciples among the gathering crowds seems to indicate that people loved to talk with Jesus. It was a coup to have a quiet dinner with him as Martha and Mary and Lazarus often did. At times, it could be challenging to talk with Jesus, to be engaged by him as the apostles discovered time and again. Children wanted to get to him to talk—even if the adults thought Jesus was too busy or too concerned with "adult" matters. His mother, Mary, clearly sought time with him, and we can only imagine what Jesus and Joseph discussed in those apprentice days.

Both men and women seemed drawn not only to tell Jesus of their need or desire, but also to ask their questions, to complain about others, to make apparently ridiculous suggestions. The gospels reveal how Jesus really modeled a way of being with his Abba and with other human beings. And the gospels suggest that there were times when, in Jesus' company, people were drawn to quiet and a contemplative presence.

◊ Do you have a longing now to be a compassionate contemplative? Or are you reserving that for the future?

◊ What has been your experience of talking with Jesus?

◊ How comfortable are you when your prayer experience of conversation with Jesus includes or leads to a quiet presence with God?

Colloquy as Conversation

C olloquy allows one to share with God one's thoughts, feelings, questions and desires with full confidence that one is heard by God. There is no age limit to being "a seeker." For some, the seeking manifests itself in dissatisfaction with one's prayer or one's relationship with Jesus and a desire to find another way, a way that captures one's person in all its ups and downs. For Ignatius, the prayer of "colloquy" was always an aspect of one's ever-growing intimacy with God so it is always appropriate. This might be the time to incorporate an intimate conversation with Jesus or "colloquy" into your prayer routine.

According to the light of God's grace given to me, I beg that I might come to know Jesus as the pattern for my own living and so be able to draw close to him. I close the prayer period with the Our Father.

Sp. Ex. 109[24]

According to the different aspects which I may focus upon at any one time within the prayer period, I respond accordingly, for example, to Mary, Joseph, Jesus, God the Father. Perhaps there is little to say because this style of contemplation is often more a "being with" experience than a word-response. I bring the period of prayer to a close with an Our Father.

Sp. Ex. 117[25]

Moments to Remember

As you recover memories or think of praying about the Seasons of your life—with nature's seasons as the background—it may seem daunting or even a bit frightening. Befriending one's imagination can seem risky. We've all known moments of loneliness in our lives and have perhaps at times felt overwhelmed by the emotions which a memory or imagining stirred in us. And there have been times when we have been bursting with desire to share some news or to ask a question. At all those times, we have known how significant a friend is. That knowledge is the human grounding for taking up the practice of Christian prayer of talking with Jesus as a friend.

◊ Do you remember a special conversation you had with Jesus? Does the memory of that conversation return to you sometimes? When?

◊ What challenges and what comforts have your conversations with Jesus held for you—and perhaps for Jesus?

Developing Your Own Conversation With Jesus

*T*hese Ignatian reflections confirm that your prayer is uniquely yours! There is no "one way" or "better way" of praying. Ignatius wisely understood this truth when he reflected on his own varied experiences in prayer at Manresa and when he offered direction to women and men. Indeed, *The Spiritual Exercises* are a classic text offering many ways of praying! Colloquy is one way—simple and intimate.

This prayer form may confirm a method of prayer which you have used throughout your life during informal as well as formal times of prayer. Colloquy also seems to be a wonderful vehicle for capturing one's awareness and experience at the end of a day. As we share our gratitude, our sorrow, our wonderment with Jesus, we allow God to give us new hope for another day, especially a day lived in a world with a scarcity of hope.

Spending time with Jesus in silence and in conversation is as old as Christian prayer. It has been the choice of women and men in every era of human history. We have all heard enough stories of the lives of other persons to know that spending time with Jesus in silence and in conversation "works" at any age. "We only devote periods of quiet time to the things or the people whom we love; and here we are speaking of the God whom we love, a God who wishes to speak to us. Because of this love, we can take as much time as we need...." (*Pope Francis*[26]) Surely, it can be a significant component of our journey as we age with consciousness and attentiveness to the ways of God in our life—its past as well as its present. Below, we offer some suggestions for placing one's prayer within the context of Jesus' mode of conversation and invite you to consider incorporating this "colloquy conversation" into your prayer throughout the book.

The following general suggestions may also encourage you as you start your own conversation with Jesus:

+ Pause with the awareness or question or emotion that has come to you as you reflected with the particular set of questions during that time of prayer—or that day.

+ Take that as the starting point for your conversation with Jesus.

+ Use your own words and style of communication. Use the amount of time that seems appropriate to you for the conversation.

+ Allow time and space for Jesus to respond —perhaps with a new awareness, with compassion, with delight or humor, with a question, with one of his words or stories in scripture.

+ Active conversation may gradually yield to a silent presence of two friends. Each will bring to that silent presence a new understanding of the other.

Discernment: Spirit-Filled Memories and Choices

How can I respond to a God so good to me and surrounding me with the goodness of holy men and women and the wonderful gifts of creation? All I can do is give thanks, wondering at God's forgiving love, which continues to give me life up to this moment.

Sp. Ex. 61[27]

Nothing is more practical than finding God, that is, than falling in love in a quite absolute, final way. What you are in love with, what seizes your imagination, will affect everything. It will decide what will get you out of bed in the morning, what you will do with your evenings, how you spend your weekends, what you read, what you know that breaks your heart, and what amazes you -with joy and gratitude. Fall in love, stay in love, and it will decide everything.

Pedro Arrupe, SJ[28]

"Spirit-filled Memories and Choices"

*T*his section invites consideration of the active role of the Spirit not only in one's memories of the past, but also in one's current decisions and actions. The text points to the important process of "reflection on experience" as a way of noticing the living and active Word of God spoken to us in our lives. It offers suggestions for prayer to become more attentive to the Spirit in one's daily life and decisions. It links our attentiveness to our role in extending the Reign of God.

◊ What have you discovered as you have taken time to reflect upon your life experience?

◊ What are you noticing about the "nudging" of the Spirit in your daily life?

◊ Ponder the ways in which you have shared in extending the Reign of God with your life.

Our lives have been enriched with their many rich and diverse experiences. You have prayerfully pondered them in this book and in your life! Aging is a mystery. As we become more attentive to the Spirit in one's daily life and decisions, we recognize our attentiveness as part of our role in extending the Reign of God. Gratefully, we realize that our faith, family and friends are important God-given gifts to us. They become and are parables of God's love for us as we continue to journey through the seasons of our lives.

Memories hold a fascination for us. Collected in scrapbooks, autobiographies, diaries, letters and family pictures, videos of all sorts, memories continually invite us to return to a special season, event or person in our lives. Revisiting those seasons, events and persons is more than an exercise in nostalgia. It is the important action of remembering a moment of grace, a moment in which God was present and active in our lives, loving us beyond measure. The gift in some memories is immediately apparent to us. Sometimes, however, it is only with timely revisiting of the special season, event or person that its gift quality becomes evident to us.

Ignatius drew upon this human tendency to revisit experiences when, in offering suggestions for prayer in *The Spiritual Exercises*, he encouraged a prayer of repetition. It is as if he knew that we miss the full import of the generosity of God as we pray and as we rush through our daily lives. In the prayer of repetition, we return to an experience where we recognized the action of God. We return either because we were mysteriously drawn and held there or because we felt within ourselves deep, or even subtle, resistance to what God was saying to us at that time. Ignatius knew

that God's unconditional love is always being revealed to us at progressively deeper levels of our being. That progressive revelation of God's love in our lives brings who we are into fuller clarity for us. As Nan C. Merrill observes, "Wisdom grows in us season by season; and may take a lifetime; yet, You love us all and grant us free will to take our own time to choose our own way."[29]

◊ What has been the gift which you have experienced as you have remembered your life?

◊ What have you discovered about the amazing action of God within human experience?

◊ How is your gratitude deepening and grounding new hope in you?

As we age, we may question how important our decisions are or even label them as unimportant. However, every free choice—whether large or small—is of significance and contributes to the unfolding of the Reign of God.

In death and judgment a person's naked reality is manifest. Death is no mere superficial change nor is judgment only an external reaction to one's actions during life. At death and judgment the personal condition a person has chosen for oneself is completed and made final. True, this final self-determination is achieved in dialogue with or against God, and would be impossible without God's free creation and gratuitous grace. Nor can we forget that freedom never totally determines any concrete life-situation. Other determinants inevitably enter each individual decision. But none of this alters what is to the Christian a self-evident fact: that freedom enables one to determine oneself irrevocably, to be for all eternity what one has chosen to make oneself. In one's freedom, a person is one's own burden and responsibility. Freedom is creative, and its creature is the human person—in one's own final disposition of oneself. A person is essentially a freedom-event. As established by God, and in one's very nature, one is unfinished. One does not live in some ethereal and pure essence but freely determines one's own everlasting nature and bears ultimate responsibility for it.

"Man is what he chooses to be" by Karl Rahner, SJ[30]

Perhaps gradually, and maybe even with deep suffering, we become convinced that God's providence has filled our lives. We see that gift while at the very same time we see how our own choices and actions may have set up roadblocks to God's action for ourselves or for others. The resulting awareness of the various patterns of thought, feeling and action that we carry into all our interactions often becomes the impetus for new choices. Basic to the new choices will be the awareness, not only of the prevailing patterns within us and our choices, but also—perhaps for the first time in my adult life—a renewed recognition that I have a choice. God's gift of my freedom to choose is seen for the profound gift that it is. And we begin to grasp the significance of the small things: the hidden choices to act for justice, to offer a kindness, to accept another's kindness, to be there for others in the soon-to-be forgotten moments. How have your daily choices become more evident to you?

◊ What reminds you to ask for the help and guidance of the Spirit as you make choices?

◊ Pause to rejoice in your awareness of the unfolding plan of God in your life.

God's love clarifies our identity and offers us continual hope for who we can become—at any age. In our daily worlds, we savor our independence and, at times, mistake that independence for our best use of God's gift of human freedom. Gradually, with the help of our memories of how God has acted in the past, we can be more trusting that God is at work. God's action is now freeing our hearts and minds from those attitudes, dispositions, memories or imaginings that can block our hearts and minds. We understand how those patterns can be preventing us from becoming the free and generous persons God calls us to be. It may become more evident to us what co-operation with God's action looks and feels like and how to be more of a collaborator with God.

God's presence in us and with us at times of both suffering and joy evokes the responses we call "faith," "hope" and "love." Again and again, we experience ourselves called to be "free from" blocks or attachments in order to be "free for" and available for God's action in our lives now. Our choices become more free of the clutter of mixed motives and we find a new peace and harmony in our lives.

As we age, not only does our personal identity become clearer to us, but our ways of acting and choosing take on a more integrated quality. Hopefully, long years of pondering the word of God begin to find a new and more consistent expression in our lives. There may still be puzzles or pain, but there is focused direction in our days. This disposition of interior freedom and trust in the providence of God becomes the solid grounding for our conversations with others. We join the story of women and men of every age whose conversations and decisions have helped to extend the Reign of God among the people and circumstances of their era. Our prayer and reflection on the seasons of our lives yields not only gratitude and hope, but also a new desire and will to be God's instrument in unveiling the Reign of God among us.

◊ As a result of reflecting upon your life, what is clearer to you about your true freedom?

◊ How would you now describe your basic identity before God?

◊ What in the Christian story is helping you to integrate the many aspects of your self and your life and to grow in faith, hope and love?

PART III

THE SEASONS:
THE PARABLES OF OUR LIVES

Entering the Seasons

*W*hen the pace of life slows a bit, or we find ourselves in a transition triggered by a birthday celebration, the life-long adventure of conversion and deepening of our relationship with God takes on a different quality. The challenge may seem even greater because the invitations of God may have a more delicate and subtle quality than those earlier in one's life. The response, too, may take on a more delicate and humble quality. But God is still the One inviting and we are still in charge of our choices of how to respond. Through it all, God heals and integrates the many strands of our lives. Above all, what becomes clear to us, as it was to Ignatius, is that all is gift!

God's desire to be with us as the Abiding Presence of the Spirit of the Risen Christ takes on new significance for us as we move forward on our journey. That amazing reality of our Christian faith — the Abiding Presence of the Spirit of the Risen Christ — is the consoling context for prayer in each of the seasons. Even as we look back in memory, the Spirit leads us forward with the help of perspective which the life-death-resurrection of Jesus offers to those memories. We experience at new depths the God who has always been with us in these moments we now remember.

"The world is charged with the grandeur of God" is the way the poet Gerard Manley Hopkins, SJ, expressed it. The four seasons are rich in detail, often challenging and surprising us by the powerful activity within them. Imagining the seasons of the natural world as God's parables, as God's way of revealing not only God's grandeur, but also the Divine presence and activity there, encourages us. It invites not only our openness to the investigations of science, but also to the stretching and expanding properties of belief.

Viewing Life as Parable

*J*esus' parables are known for their surprising endings and call to conversion. Viewing one's life through the lens of parable allows us to welcome the questions, the aspects that seemed so puzzling or mysterious until we discovered God at work even in and through us and our lives!

In Part III, seasons and parables offer a backdrop for God's actions in our entire lives and, in the case of these pages, offer ways of "getting at" the meaning and purpose of all the segments of our lives. The seasons are used as the broad framework within which to look again and carefully listen once more to the parables of our daily lives. Discovering within one's own unfolding life the surprising action, invitation and teaching of God centers us. It opens the way for a new response to God's gracious presence with us now. For Jesus, parables were poignant and perceptive observations of the real world. He used parables as ways of moving his followers to new daily attitudes and actions in extending the Reign of God. Considering our lives as God's parables challenges us to be mission-oriented people through every stage of life.

As you begin to use this section, spend some time considering which of the four seasons most clearly images the current personal season of your life. For example, are you living an autumn time in which you are gathering the fruits and wisdom of many years of authentic living? In that instance, it might be helpful to go directly to "Autumn" and make your way through that section of the book. Or is there a hint of newness in your life which might lead you to begin praying with "Spring?" The following brief phrases may also offer enough hints to help you decide on your starting point. Of course, it will be fine to begin at the beginning!

Springtime carries in its weather such promise of newness even as it bangs against the hard, uncracked surfaces of earth—and of us.

Summer seems lush in so many ways; one can hardly keep up with the growth and change. And still one can be stunned by the ferocity of heat and storms.

Autumn has that funny combination of new beginnings offered by the civic world around us and harvests which mark the completion and endings of crops, planned action and accomplishments.

Winter can be starkly beautiful, darkly ominous, in a hurry to explode in celebration or in the uncontrollable ways of Mother Earth, Sister Death and our Risen Friend.

PART III The Seasons: The Parables Of Our Lives

Moving Through the Seasons

A fruitful way of moving through "The Seasons" may be to imagine that one is walking through them not alone, but with Jesus as one's steady companion. You might want to use your imagination and take a walk with Jesus through the seasons of your life! Teresa of Avila described her own prayer by saying, "I walk and I talk with my good Friend, Jesus." The Risen Jesus has been walking with us through our lives so it is not a far stretch to turn to the Risen Lord now as we reflect and remember how our life has unfolded. We may discover, as the disciples on the road to Emmaus did, more of the presence and action of God that was really going on throughout the seasons of our lives.

This part of our aging journey seems to offer something for everyone! Your own wisdom after long years of prayer and encounter with God will guide you as you make your way through Spring, Summer, Autumn, Winter. Ignatius would remind you to "stay where you are finding fruit." There is no schedule to be kept or goals to achieve when one is gazing upon the reality of one's life in the loving presence of God.

The scripture references to parables remind us that Jesus used parables to teach us about ourselves, our relationships and our world. The mysteries of the Reign of God are like the air we breathe — always present, but not seen except with the eyes of faith. We need to get inside Jesus' stories and parables to understand them. They are stories which give us space in which to walk around and find our own story. We find our place in the parable through the use of our imagination. With our imagination we can make the connections between the mystery of Christ and our own personal mystery. It is here where Christ's story merges and meshes with ours. Thus in "living the gospel message" our own lives become a parable. We are invited and challenged at any age to have our lives become a parable advancing the Reign of God.

A Mosaic for Praying the Seasons as a Parable of Your Life

*T*he content in each of the following sections will probably resonate with some periods or experiences in your life. It is our hope that making any season your starting point will allow you to move with the two-fold intent of the book: to become ever more grateful for what your life has held and to allow that gratitude to be a foundation for your deepening hope as you move into the future to which God calls you. Gratitude and hope combine to deepen the trust that is called forth from us as we continue to surrender to God's mysterious ways.

At the beginning of each season section, there is a collection of images and memories listed as reminders of God's action in and through our imagination and memory. These are images which may surface and evoke old memories and new images for your life. They are not exhaustive and may need your favorites to be added to the list to make them real for you. We are fully aware that there are many different geographical climates in God's beautiful and fragile world. If you live in a one-season climate feel free to use your memory and imagination to make your reflection local!

Ignatian prayer encourages attention to memory and imagination as ways God uses to reach us and to draw us into a deeper relationship. The list of images at the beginning of each season may begin that new reverencing of your memories. They give clues to your life parables. Those carriers of grace highlight some of the ways that God touched you with an invitation at an earlier time of your life.

A phrase from that listing of images and memories is repeated as particular sections for prayer begin. Once again, they have a simple purpose: to serve as a way of encouraging your attentiveness to God's action within your memories and imagination. The title of that section tries to orient your attention so that the questions will make a bit more sense.

The Gospel parables which begin each season are the timeless reminders of God's ways. We hear the familiar words and know they do speak in our day. They invite us to consider our lives, too, as parables with the elements of mystery and surprise and challenge. They draw us to the life-giving Word of God for nourishment and confirmation of God's invitations and challenges in our lives.

Listen carefully to His words. As Jesus spoke to the crowds, He now speaks to us!

...Let anyone with ears to hear listen!

Mark 4:9

...Jesus told the crowds all these things in parables; without a parable he told them nothing.

Matthew 13:34

Moments to Remember

...But as for that in the good soil, these are the ones who, when they hear the word, hold it fast in an honest and good heart, and bear fruit with patient endurance.

Luke 8:13

...Therefore every scribe who has been trained for the kingdom of heaven is like the master of a household who brings out of his treasure what is new and what is old.

Matthew 13:53

The gospels are filled with Jesus' questions — simple, penetrating, probing, evocative, thought-provoking. In the Sermon on the Mount, he addressed the questions to all in the crowds, but at other times, his questions are directed to individuals. We know from experience how those questions can bring us to new awareness in our relationship with God, with others and with ourselves. As human persons, we are helped by questions. They are not just to focus our thought process or organize the wealth within our mind and heart. The pursuit of them often carries us to unexpected places where God awaits us with new wisdom and desire.

Each section, therefore, in the Seasons contains some reflection questions which we hope will be the occasion of your coming to new understandings about your life — its past, its present and its future. They focus one's prayer and reflection on the gifts which an unfolding life has held as well as upon the longings which are moving within. At times, the questions may stir the imagination to consider the ordinary—either past or present—in new ways. Any of them may carry God's new invitation for today. They are not exhaustive so they may also serve as a springboard to your further reflections and prayer.

As you make your way through the sections for prayer, be free to use as many or as few of the questions as prove to be helpful for you. They are offered to launch your reflection and prayer and perhaps to offer a new orientation for viewing events of your life. At times the questions may lead you to memories and images of times in your life. When that happens, it is an invitation to pause. It's not just a trip down memory lane. God may have a new word or new perspective on that memory to offer you today. *"If today you hear God's voice, harden not your hearts."* (Psalm 95:8)

There are words of wisdom figures—whether scripture writer, poet, saint or well-known figure —which are also gifts to us as we move forward in our lives. They are quotations from a variety of persons throughout human history who also reflected upon their experience, seeking understanding, direction, and encouragement, meaning and hope. They remind us of the timeless work of memory and imagination in other persons who also reflected upon their experiences. They may inspire or confirm or even offer a new invitation. You may want to add a few favorite quotes which you have remembered from earlier times in your life. The gift of wisdom develops over a lifetime.

Finally, there is a reminder to spend some time in a "colloquy conversation" each time you pray the Seasons. Ignatius wisely said, "…you might want to pray in words such as this…" Some days we are not sure how to begin that conversation with Jesus or Mary or our loving God. Identifying the awareness that has come to you in that prayer—or in that day—might be the starting point for your colloquy. We have offered a simple colloquy after the reflection questions in each Season to help you begin your own quiet colloquy time. They may become your prayer or they may just remind you to have that intimate conversation with Jesus. Above all, use them only until you feel at home in your own way of "colloquy" prayer.

The accumulated lived experience of those who pray with this book will surely describe many of the unfolding parables and conversations in the lives of faithful women and men of this era. God's word for God's people is new every day. Bringing free and discerning hearts to prayer and relationships at this time of life may be one of our ways of extending the Reign of God in our 21st century world.

Moments
to Remember

Yellow crocuses pushing thru the soil;
geese migrating in flight formation;
dirty snow washed away by spring rains;
teacher conferences;
return of robins;
March Madness;
tax deadlines;
cherry blossom time;
sweet scent of magnolia trees;
The Masters;
ice chunks floating downstream;
spring fever;
graduation ceremonies;
fragrance of lilacs;
Spring, a season of promise.

Ponder these images and
memories as you begin
praying with Spring

SPRING SEASONS OF MY LIFE

Again he began to teach beside the sea...many things in parables. "Listen! A sower went out to sow. And as he sowed, some seed fell on the path, and the birds came and ate it up. Other seed fell on rocky ground, where it did not have much soil, and it sprang up quickly, since it had no depth of soil. And when the sun rose, it was scorched; and since it had no root, it withered away. Other seed fell among thorns, and the thorns grew up and choked it, and it yielded no grain. Other seed fell into good soil and brought forth grain, growing up and increasing and yielding thirty and sixty and a hundredfold." And he said, "Let anyone with ears to hear listen!"

Parable of the Sower, Mark 4:1–9

SPRING 1
Memories: *"Spring, a season of promise"*

Making Way for the New

◊ Where in your life is there new growth?

◊ In what ways are you aware of being transformed?

◊ What puts a "spring in your step?" What is the "song in your heart" that delights or comforts you?

◊ What helps you to balance and keep in perspective "new ways" and "old ways?"

◊ How are people helping you to make these new adjustments?

Moments to Remember

Wisdom Words

> Let me seek you in longing and long for you in seeking. Let me find you in love, and love you in finding.
>
> *St. Ambrose*[31]

> You will do well to be attentive to the Word, as to a lamp shining in a dark place, until day dawns and the morning star rises in your hearts.
>
> *2 Peter 1:19*

> Joy is the infallible sign of the presence of God.
>
> *Pierre Teilhard de Chardin, SJ*[32]

Colloquy

In your own words, simply ask Jesus for the grace to be fertile for any seed of grace you may need at this moment in your life.

SPRING 2

Images: *"Yellow crocuses pushing thru the soil"*

Awareness and Wonder

◊ How did the Spirit guide your memory or imagination in the quiet ordinary moments of today?

◊ What are you discovering when you reverence times of quiet?

◊ What kind of nourishment do you need now for that awareness to grow?

◊ What life experiences move you to pray with wonder — whether before the small and delicate or the grand and majestic?

Moments to Remember

◊ What ways have you found to live in the present, grateful for and savoring the present moment?

Wisdom Words

A Granddaughter's Gifts
by Edwin F. Block[33]

Besides the artwork on the fridge;
besides the hugs;
the gift she brings: a sense of time
slowed down, to match a three-year-old;
a calm and inner quiet, peace.

A thing of beauty is a joy forever: Its loveliness increases; it will never pass into nothingness.

John Keats[34]

The world will never starve for want of wonders; but only for want of wonder.... Gratitude is happiness doubled by wonder.

G.K. Chesterton[35]

By virtue of Creation, and still more the Incarnation, nothing here below is profane for those who know how to see.

Pierre Teilhard de Chardin, SJ[36]

Colloquy

Spend some quiet time reflecting on what you have felt when beholding a breath-taking sunset or a new infant.

SPRING 3
Memories: *"Sudden Spring Rains"*

Grounded in God's Peace

◊ What area of your life holds uncertainty?

◊ What routines help you to stay grounded and interiorly free in the midst of uncertainty?

◊ What actions yield peace and trust in the face of the feelings of uncertainty?

◊ How can you link your uncertainty and waiting in daily life with your trust and longing for God?

Wisdom Words

God awaits us every instant in our action, in the work of the moment. There is a sense in which he is at the tip of my pen, my spade, my brush, my needle — of my heart and my thought.

Pierre Teilhard de Chardin, SJ[37]

Only in love can I find you, my God. In love the gates of my soul spring open, allowing me to breathe a new air of freedom and forget my own petty self. In love my whole being streams forth out of the rigid confines of narrowness and anxious self-assertion, which make me a prisoner of my own poverty emptiness. In love all the powers of my soul flow out toward you, wanting never more to return, but to lose themselves completely in you, since by your love you are the inmost center of my heart, closer to me than I am to myself.

Karl Rahner, SJ[38]

Genuine freedom is not the right to do whatever we want, but the liberty to do what we ought.

John Paul II[39]

Occasionally in life there are those moments of unutterable fulfillment which cannot be completely explained by those symbols called words. Their meanings can only be articulated by the inaudible language of the heart.

Martin Luther King, Jr.[40]

Colloquy

The Lord invites you to turn to Him in all circumstances. Talk to Him about any area of uncertainty or waiting which you experience in your life.

SPRING 4
Memories: *"Graduation ceremonies"*

The Gift of Companionship

◊ What has God's providential care for you already taught you?

◊ How has your wisdom and interior freedom been enriched by the varied experiences and friendships of your life?

◊ Who are the people whom you trust to be with you in your current planning? Have you invited them into your confidence?

◊ While planning is always limited by some unknown factors, are there steps you can take, seeds you can sow, to plan for the next phases of your life while also surrendering to God's providential care?

Moments to Remember

◊ What person or event seems to be asking for a more important place in your life? What might the hope and peace, or discouragement and fear, occasioned by this invitation signal to you?

◊ What has spring gardening taught you that can support you as you age? Would a walk past a garden with sprouts of new growth of flowers and weeds be an encouraging activity today?

Wisdom Words

I've learned that people will forget what you said, people will forget what you did, but people will never forget how you made them feel.

Maya Angelou[41]

Let nothing trouble you. Let nothing frighten you. Everything passes, God never changes. Patience obtains all. Whoever has God wants for nothing. God alone is enough.

St. Teresa of Avila[42]

To love another person is to see the face of God.

Victor Hugo[43]

The Spirit is at Work transfiguring the power of domination into the power that is love....We do not become related when we love one another; we are already related...we are not free to choose that we will be related, but we choose how we will relate, that is, whether our relationships will be characterized by love or hate, healing or destruction, fear or trust.

Kathleen Fischer[44]

Colloquy

Take a few minutes now to thank God for your friends. Ask Jesus to bless them whether they are still living on earth or now with Him in Heaven. End this simple prayer by thanking your friend Jesus for His faithful presence in your life.

SPRING 5
Images: *"Dirty snow washed away by spring rains"*

Letting Go

◊ What are your thoughts, feelings and memories about your many possessions?

◊ What joy or pain surfaces when you gaze at treasured mementos? Are these invitations to revisit an event or relationship in your life?

◊ When possessions begin to seem like "so much stuff," it might be time for "spring-cleaning." How might you plan to enrich others, or the recyclers, with both your "treasured possessions" and your "stuff?"

◊ How can limits of money, of space, of energy, of time be good limits to embrace?

◊ To what story of Jesus do you turn when you experience limits or loss? How does this enhance your growing dependence on God?

Wisdom Words

The more clearly we can focus our attention on the wonders and realities of the universe around us, the less taste we shall have for destruction.

Rachel Carson[45]

...do not worry about your life.... Look at the birds of the air; they neither sow nor reap...and yet your... Father feeds them. Are you not of more value than they?...can any of you by worrying add a single hour to your span of life? Consider the lilies of the field, how they grow;...Solomon in all his glory was not clothed like one of these.... do not worry, saying, 'What will we eat?' or 'What will we drink?' or 'What will we wear?' Your Father knows that you need all these things....strive first for the kingdom of God...and all these things will be given to you as well. So do not worry.

Matthew 6:25–33

Simplicity is the ultimate sophistication.

Leonardo da Vinci[46]

God asks everything of us, yet at the same time he offers everything to us.

Pope Francis[47]

Colloquy

In simple, plain words speak to Jesus about whatever has surfaced in your memory and imagination when you pondered these words and questions about letting go.

Images: *"The gentle and slow greening of trees"*

New Growth Among the Weeds

◊ What wake-up call to a new perspective is God giving you in these days?

◊ What new personal needs are you beginning to realize are invitations to change?

◊ How are weaknesses beginning to appear as strengths in your life?

◊ How can an attitude of entitlement block your awareness, thus dimming your humble gratitude and acceptance of God's generous love?

Moments to Remember

◊ As, or if, you struggle with patience and forgiveness, what relief do you find in the discovery that God continues to call you to conversion and assures you of loving mercy?

Wisdom Words

Seek out that particular mental attribute which makes you feel most deeply and vitally alive, along with which comes the inner voice which says, 'This is the real me,' and when you have found that attitude, follow it.

William James[48]

Have patience with all things, but chiefly have patience with yourself; every day begin the task anew.

Saint Francis de Sales[49]

See everything, overlook a great deal, and correct a little.

Pope John XXIII[50]

The Gospel offers us the image of Simeon and Anna as two older persons who hope in the Lord's promises and then, when perhaps least expected, see them at last fulfilled. Simeon and Anna are models of a spirituality for the elderly. They point to the centrality of prayer; indeed, the prayer of grandparents is a great grace for families and for the Church. In prayer, they thank the Lord for his blessings, otherwise so often unacknowledged; intercede for the hopes and needs of the young; and lift up to God the memory and sacrifices of past generations. The purifying power of faith and prayer also helps us to find the wisest way to teach the young that the true meaning of life is found in self-sacrificing love and concern for others. Young people listen to their grandparents!

Pope Francis[51]

Colloquy

In your imagination, kneel before Jesus on the Cross. Be there with Him. Look into His eyes and thank Him for specific ways in which you have experienced His love and mercy in your life.

God's Grandeur
by Gerard Manley Hopkins, SJ[52]

THE WORLD is charged with the grandeur of God.
It will flame out, like shining from shook foil;
It gathers to a greatness, like the ooze of oil
Crushed. Why do men then now not reck his rod?
Generations have trod, have trod, have trod;
And all is seared with trade;
bleared, smeared with toil;
And wears man's smudge
and shares man's smell: the soil
Is bare now, nor can foot feel, being shod.

And for all this, nature is never spent;
There lives the dearest freshness deep down things;
And though the last lights off the black West went
Oh, morning, at the brown brink eastward, springs—
Because the Holy Ghost over the bent
World broods with warm breast
and with ah! bright wings.

Moments
to Remember

Picnics;
crowded beaches;
Fourth of July fireworks;
family trips;
weddings;
the taste of fresh tomatoes;
dancing fire flies;
gazing at the stars;
butterflies flitting from flower to flower;
gentle rains;
smell of newly mown grass;
fishing in the early dawn;
buzz of mosquitoes;
thunder and the crack of lightning;
roar of motorcycles;
Farmers Market;
sounds of the ocean;
summer sunsets.

Ponder these images and
memories as you begin
praying with Summer

SUMMER SEASONS OF MY LIFE

He put before them another parable: "The kingdom of heaven is like a mustard seed that someone took and sowed in his field; it is the smallest of all the seeds, but when it has grown it is the greatest of shrubs and becomes a tree, so that the birds of the air come and make nests in its branches." He told them another parable: "The kingdom of heaven is like yeast that a woman took and mixed in with three measures of flour until all of it was leavened." Jesus told the crowds all these things in parables; without a parable he told them nothing.

Parables of Mustard Seed and Yeast,
Matthew 13:31–35

SUMMER 1
Memories: *"The taste of fresh tomatoes"*

Energy and Activity

◊ What is stirred in you when you engage in conversation with younger women and men during family or neighborhood gatherings? How are you moved to pray for future generations?

◊ What is the focus of your summer travel? Can good books or films or the internet be a new way of "traveling the world" when air fares are too high or your energy too low?

◊ What areas of public life stir vigorous opinions in you? Do you know why they do?

◊ What sports events do you enjoy now? Do you focus on the scores, the stories of the players or on both?

◊ What story from the life of Jesus reminds you that God is not a scorekeeper?

Wisdom Words

Never lose an opportunity of seeing anything that is beautiful; for beauty is God's handwriting—a wayside sacrament. Welcome it in every fair face, in every fair sky, in every fair flower, and thank God for it as a cup of blessing.

Ralph Waldo Emerson[53]

...the Lord has taken the initiative, he has loved us first and therefore we can move forward, boldly take the initiative, go out to others, seek those who have fallen away, stand at the crossroads and welcome the outcast.

Pope Francis[54]

Talent develops in quiet places, character in the full current of human life.

Johann Wolfgang von Goethe[55]

Contemplation is basically a social matter. Solitude has its own special work: a deepening of awareness that the world needs....True solitude is deeply aware of the world's needs. It does not hold the world at arm's length....Contemplation...becomes a reservoir of spiritual vitality that pours itself out in the most telling social action.

Thomas Merton[56]

Colloquy

"Jesus advanced in wisdom, knowledge and grace before God and God's people." Spend some quiet prayer time with Jesus. Ask Him for the grace to know where you also are being called to changes in attitudes or patterns of action.

SUMMER 2
Images: *"Gazing at the stars"*

Ordinary Days Made New

◊ What are your memories of "lazy summer days?"

◊ What happens to your "world" and your role in it as you ponder the magnitude and magnificence of contemporary scientific discoveries?

◊ What have the many global and environmental issues of this era revealed to you about the significance of your personal and communal choices?

◊ What reminds you to entrust the particular global needs of this time to the Creating God of all times?

◊ What events and people are forming your attitudes toward the current season of your own life?

◊ What attitude of Jesus would you like to develop within yourself now?

Wisdom Words

Yesterday is history. Tomorrow is a mystery. And today? Today is a gift. That's why we call it the present.

Babatunde Olatunji[57]

There is only one thing necessary: to act justly, love tenderly and walk humbly with your God.

Micah 6:8

Do you realize the privilege of giving to God? It is yours at every moment.

Cornelia Connelly[58]

...the wonder is that...there is beauty at all, grace gratuitous...like mockingbird's free fall. Beauty itself is the fruit of the creator's exuberance....

Annie Dillard[59]

Colloquy

Lord, the world is awesome and filled with Your beauty. Give me a greater reverence for its fragility. Touch my heart with gratitude as I ponder Your gift of on-going creation.

SUMMER 3
Memories: *"Human Adventures"*

Rituals and Celebrations

◊ How do the celebration of national holidays, family birthdays and anniversaries move you? Perhaps to prayer and gratitude or with deep emotion?

◊ If you are often not at peace with yourself or in many circumstances, what could be lurking in the midst of the agitation?

◊ Can you bring your distress to God and ask for the gift of interior peace — even if it will mean letting go of something or being called to a change of heart?

◊ What has the sadness of personal or social sin brought into your life? What helps you to reach through sadness to peace and more life and love?

◊ When you think of God's mercy, what images come to mind? Do you remember an experience of God's mercy?

◊ How is God's mercy shifting your perspective and giving you new images of forgiveness? What daily activity can keep you attuned to God's mercy?

◊ Consider having a conversation with Jesus about the desire you have to forgive yourself and others.

Wisdom Words

> People are like stained-glass windows. They sparkle and shine when the sun is out, but when the darkness sets in, their true beauty is revealed only if there is a light from within.
>
> *Elisabeth Kubler-Ross*[60]

> Everybody is unique. Do not compare yourself with anybody else lest you spoil God's curriculum.
>
> *Baal Shem Tov*[61]

> Love is the most powerful and still the most unknown energy in the world.
>
> *Pierre Teilhard de Chardin, SJ*[62]

> I prefer a Church which is bruised, hurting and dirty because it has been out on the streets, rather than a Church which is unhealthy from being confined and from clinging to its own security.
>
> *Pope Francis*[63]

Colloquy

Jesus, You knew the joys and sorrows of family life. So did Your mother! Did you ever talk to her about her missing Joseph? By the way, I am happy to hear that You wanted Your friends to "let the children come" to You. Lord, please take care of children, especially those who are homeless, hungry or abused. And please continue to show Your mercy to me, another one of Your children.

SUMMER 4
Images: *"Picnics"*

A Growing Friendship

◊ Consider reading one of the four gospels from beginning to end. The gospel of Mark or Luke might be good ones to start your journey through the gospels.

◊ What always strikes you about Jesus when you hear or read the gospels?

◊ What new awareness about Jesus occurs to you when you recall that he went to picnics and weddings, walked by the sea and fled into the mountains to be alone, knew about leaven and copper coins as well as about the signs given by the skies?

◊ Have you ever talked with Jesus about his experiences of confinement—in Mary's womb, in a small village, in prison, in a fishing boat, in just one small country?

◊ How might such a conversation influence your thoughts and feelings about the value of confinement and your particular life-circumstance?

Wisdom Words

I don't know Who—or what—put the questions, I don't know when it was put. I don't even remember answering. But at some moment I did answer Yes to Someone—or Something—and from that hour I was certain that existence is meaningful and that, therefore, my life, in self-surrender, had a goal.

Dag Hammarskjold[64]

Only when I saw the Earth from space, in all its ineffable beauty and fragility, did I realize that humankind's most urgent task is to cherish and preserve it for future generations.

Sigmund Jahn[65]

The joy of the gospel fills the hearts and lives of all who encounter Jesus.

Pope Francis[66]

Because we all share this planet earth, we have to learn to live in harmony and peace with each other and with nature. That is not just a dream, but a necessity. We are dependent on each other in so many ways that we can no longer live in isolated communities and ignore what is happening outside those communities.

The Dalai Lama[67]

Colloquy

Jesus, You are becoming more real to me as a person. Perhaps it is because I am so aware of my own humanity, especially when I am tired or frightened. Please help me to turn to You in those moments. I need to hear and remember Your reassuring words!

SUMMER 5
Images: *"Dancing fireflies"*

Hidden in the Ordinary

◊ What activities make up the ordinary of your life now? What call to growth is carried by the ordinary in your life?

◊ What beliefs help you when the ordinary in life seems dull, boring or tedious?

◊ What are you able to offer others as they, too, have ordinary days that may be boring and tedious?

◊ What activities from an earlier part of your life do you miss being able to do?

Moments to Remember

◊ How comfortable are you with acknowledging that you can do "this, but not that?"

◊ How can you draw upon your experience of God's presence and action at earlier times of limit to help you now?

Wisdom Words

For if we have received the love which restores meaning to our lives, how can we fail to share that love with others?

Pope Francis[68]

The best book, like the best speech, will do it all—make us laugh, think, cry and cheer —preferably in that order.

Madeleine Albright[69]

There are two ways to live your life. One is as though nothing is a miracle. The other is as though everything is a miracle.

Albert Einstein[70]

Finally I saw that worrying had come to nothing.
And gave it up. And took my old body and went
into the morning, and sang.

Mary Oliver[71]

Earth crammed with heaven, And every common
bush afire with God; But only he who sees, takes
off his shoes, The rest sit round it and pluck
blackberries...

Elizabeth Barrett Browning[72]

Colloquy

Lord, today I have a few questions about Your
life. How—besides eating—did you relax with Your
friends when You were on the road? The stories about
You never tell us things like that. I think You did
relax because You were like us in "everything but sin."
Jesus, what did You do with the very human ordinary
moments in Your life? Help me to experience Your
presence in the ordinary and hidden routine of my life.

SUMMER 6
Memories: *"Fishing in the early dawn"*

Quiet Time

◊ What is happening to your way of praying as you find a new and simpler rhythm in your life?

◊ Can you just sit still? What might happen if you did that for 15 minutes each day?

◊ What are you discovering when you reverence times of quiet? Can classical or jazz or religious music be a companion on quiet days? Are there untapped artistic gifts in you waiting to be explored?

◊ Are you aware of an invitation to trust that God is as present in stillness as in activity?

◊ Do you accept that invitation? If not, why not? Ask Mary, the mother of Jesus, to help you to be still, to wait with hope and peace.

Wisdom Words

The best and most beautiful things in the world cannot be seen, nor touched but are felt in the heart.

Helen Keller[73]

So when you come before the Lord, talk to Him if you can; if you can't, just stay there, let yourself be seen, and don't try too hard to do anything else.

Francis de Sales[74]

God is present in moments of rest and can give us in a single instant exactly what we need. Then the rest of the day can take its course, under the same effort and strain, perhaps, but in peace. And when night comes, and you look back over the day and see how fragmentary everything has been, and how much you planned that has gone undone, and all the reasons you have to be embarrassed and ashamed: just take everything exactly as it is, put it in God's hands, and leave it with God. Then you will be able to rest in God—really rest—and start the next day as a new life.

St. Teresa of the Cross (Edith Stein)[75]

Moments to Remember

Colloquy

Lord, in Your very busy days of caring for the people, You knew Your need and desire to spend some quiet time alone in prayer. Help me, Lord, to become quiet and comfortable in Your presence.

Pied Beauty
by Gerard Manley Hopkins, SJ[76]

GLORY be to God for dappled things—
For skies of couple-colour as a brinded cow;
For rose-moles all in stipple upon trout that swim;
Fresh-firecoal chestnut-falls; finches' wings;
Landscape plotted and pieced—fold, fallow, and plough;
And áll trádes, their gear and tackle and trim.

All things counter, original, spare, strange;
Whatever is fickle, freckled (who knows how?)
With swift, slow; sweet, sour; adazzle, dim;
He fathers-forth whose beauty is past change:
Praise him.

Moments to Remember

Labor Day weekend;
tailgating;
trees ablaze in riotous color;
one last round of golf;
Autumn sunsets;
the crunch of leaves underfoot;
All Saints Day;
All Souls Day;
distinctive smell of burning leaves;
harvest moon slowly emerging;
honk of geese going south;
family Thanksgiving traditions;
squirrels busily gathering nuts for the winter.

Ponder these images and
memories as you begin
praying with Autumn